T0067446

My Life's Experiences *in the* Proof *of* Psychic Phenomenon

Rev. Mary Linn Clarke

BALBOA.
PRESS
A DIVISION OF HAY HOUSE

Interior Graphics/Art Credit: Rev. Mary Linn Clarke

Balboa Press books may be ordered through booksellers or by contacting:

Balboa Press
A Division of Hay House
1663 Liberty Drive
Bloomington, IN 47403
www.balboapress.com
1 (877) 407-4847

Print information available on the last page.

ISBN: 978-1-5043-5834-7 (sc)
ISBN: 978-1-5043-5835-4 (e)

Balboa Press rev. date: 07/05/2016

Dedication

I dedicate this book to my spirit teachers, loved ones and friends.

To Laura Lynn Cassidy, in appreciation for the effort and help to put this book together.

It would have not been made possible, thank you.

Prelude

Where It All Began

Experiences I have had all throughout my sixty eight years have been contributed to the belief of the Universal Light and the works of those much higher than I beyond this earth life. At the age of thirteen, I always believed of something that was beyond the original belief system at that time.

Being a Baptist tradition, all my friends were being baptized. So, I took it upon myself to be baptized as well. The customary procedure was to be submerged into the water as the minister was holding your nose. A strange thing happened to me while under the water. I heard a voice say to me "This is not for you!" and it kept repeating over and over again. I could not hear the words that the minister was saying to me. All I knew was that this was a message, given to me.

Soon after this experience, my mother and father were introduced to a belief system of Spiritualism. This is also modernly known as Metaphysics. They had attended classes often and one day out of the blue, I asked my parents if I could go to church with them. They were never ones to push religion or belief system onto another person. They gave me free choice to choose what I wanted. The experience was quite interesting. The service was different from other churches I had been to and there were many. The other church services were never satisfying or fulfilling for me, even at that young age. I could not relate to other beliefs. I would even have discussions with ministers about certain subjects that I questioned (we won't go into that – to each his own). As the service continued, it came to the part where they gave messages to prove the continuity of life after death. The medium was the connecting link between earth and spirit world. The medium came to me, the message given was that I would be doing the same work that she was doing except on a larger scale. It would be at the age of my late thirties, which to me was as old as methuselah!

After high school, I attended college in my home town. I thought I would like to be a commercial artist (wrong). The medium was completely right. As time went on, my mother became a trance medium. Sitting in a circle in our home, we received many beautiful messages from our Spirit teachers, Master teachers and Universal teachers. My father became a very fine Healer and was trained by an old German Healer in the small spiritualist church to which we had been attending.

My parents later decided to move to Florida and once there they became long time members of another spiritualist church in the area. Finally, an opportunity came for me to go to a spiritualist college in St. Petersburg, Florida, called Harmonia College. It was founded by Dr. Enid Smith a philosophy teacher who held seven different degrees. I was very fortunate to have private tutoring. I studied under some of the finest Metaphysical teachers of that time, including Reverend Bill English and many more. Reverend Lillian D. Johnson was a teacher who would eventually became my mentor. She also taught out of Camp Chesterfield, Indiana.

This was only the beginning of my life's experiences in the proof of psychic phenomenon.

The UFO

One experience I had while attending college, was when I had to have some repairs done to my car. The garage was near a dear friend of mine, she was getting up there in her years and also knew Dr. Enid. She asked me if I would like to come over for dinner since she was only a short distance away. After dinner, my friend walked me to a bus stop because my car had to stay at the garage. On the way there, I noticed something very strange in the sky. I knew it wasn't an airplane, because it wasn't moving. Maybe a helicopter? No, you couldn't hear the propellers.

I was under the impression that this could possibly be a UFO!

I mentally projected the thought, "If you are a UFO, would you please come over to where we are standing?" All of a sudden, the object turned and moved towards us. It hovered over our heads for a minute or two. To describe the appearance, I would presume that it was about one hundred fifty feet high and round in structure with white, red and orange lights around the rim. Underneath in the center was large light surrounded by what looked to me to be chicken wire. It took a forty five degree angle and moved away. My friend and I both saw the craft as it hovered over our heads. Unfortunately, her eye sight was very poor and she could not see all that I had seen.

After leaving my friend and continuing to the bus stop, the object hovered between two trees. There was another lady standing there with me at the bus stop. I mentally projected the thought out that the lady would look up and see this object! God only knows what she would do! They seemed to pick up on my thoughts, turned sideways, moved over a trendmedous speed and was gone.

Experience Two

Psychic Surgery

One incident occurred when my mother used to have angina attacks and require four nitro glycerin tablets a day. One day a friend of ours had heard about a psychic surgeon in Georgia who had trained over seven years to develop this type of phenomenon. He would go into a cataleptic trance rigid state. He had to take it in different stages starting with a light trance, to medium, to a cataleptic state to which his spirit left his body. The spirit chemist would control his or her molecular parts of the body to produce this phenomenon.

We decided to make an appointment. We were met at the door by Reverend Bill, a down to earth and very personable person. (His story about how he got started is quite interesting as well.) We were prepared that evening for what was to take place the next day. We were awakened about six A.M. and we had to put hospital gowns on. The night before we were told to eat nothing, almost like you do if you are having an operation. We were escorted into a room where there was a type of massage table with sheets on it. A few chairs, one at the bottom of the table were his wife Nancy took notes. Reverend Bill took a chair about five feet away from the table. There was a prayer said before he went into a trance state. His spirit chemist put him into a cataleptic (rigid) state while in this trance. A spirit doctor was the diagnostician before they passed into the spirit world. There were several specialist in the band of doctors that worked with Reverend Bill.

Mom was the first to go. The diagnostician then proceeded to scan mom's body relating what he found to Nancy, who was taking notes of what the problem was. My mother, who was an RN and a surgical nurse, could relate exactly what his diagnoses was. The spirit doctor then returned back to the chair, left the body in which he was occupying. A few short minutes later, another doctor was brought into Reverend Bill's body. This was a heart specialist. He was a different personality from the diagnostician. I believe his name was Doctor Fredricks. Without going into details, mom had a closed valve. In fact, there were a few. Dr. Fredricks commenced to explain what he was doing. My mother being a surgical nurse, knew exactly what he was doing and the type of instruments he used to repair the condition. The procedure was done.

To perform a psychic surgery, the spirit doctors have to raise the etheric body up from the physical body. The etheric body is an exact duplicate of the physical body, but lighter in density. The etheric body must be healed first, then the physical body becomes whole. This the same method used when you do Therapeutic Touch healing. "We must heal the etheric body first".

Dr. Fredricks was then finished and Reverend Bill came out of the rigid trance. It took a few moments for him to come out of that type of trance. (They also did a procedure for my hemorrhoids and repaired them. I haven't had any repercussions since.) We were taken back to our room and told we would only have a light meal. We were not to get up, only to go to the bathroom. We went home the next day and mom was told not to do any lifting or bending. They treated it like a regular physical surgery.

In the end, mom lived her life quite a few years after that. She rarely had to use Nitro Glycerin, maybe one time here or there. She had felt one hundred percent better.

Experience Three

Materialization

One of the most incredible phenomena I had witnessed happened in the seventies. My mom, a few friends and I had decided to go up to Camp Silverbell in Pennsylvania. (Unfortunately, it doesn't exist now. They had wonderful teachers and much to learn.) Our group decided to go to a materialization séance with Reverend Roy Burkholder. Rev. Roy was recognized as one of the most experienced materialization mediums, bar none. We entered a room that could seat at least twenty five people. The room was darkened except for a red light in the corner of the room. It showed the direction of a cabinet, a five by five space covered with black curtains with an opening in the front of it. Rev. Roy and his door keeper entered the room. Rev. Roy took his place inside of the cabinet, while his door keeper sat outside to the left of it.

When a materialization medium goes into a very deep state of trance, his own spirit leaves the body. The Spirit Chemist draws from the mediums physical body a chemical called ectoplasm. It is drawn from the orifice and solar plexus of the body. The cabinet acts as a fortress to keep the ectoplasm in a condensed state (solid) when drawn from the medium. By the help of the chemist from the spirit world, the loved ones can materialize. Sometimes in a solid form (rare) or a vapor form depending on the progression and experience of the spirit that utilizes the substance. They also use the mediums vocal cords to communicate. The red light does not destroy ectoplasm, while pure white light disintegrates and breaks up the ectoplasm.

There were many spirit loved ones, guides, teachers and masters that made their appearance. Finally, it came to my turn. The entity that materialized from the cabinet was a very high soul. He came and stood outside who and of course I knew who he was. He was my spirit chemist and physical doctor teacher. He told me what he was about to do for me and not to get excited. He almost stood in full form, spoke a few words to me and then suddenly disintegrated right down to the floor. The ectoplasm was seen as it was drawn back in to the medium's solar plexus. It was a demonstration of materialization that I had never witnessed. It was very exciting to me.

A few months later, Rev. Roy was holding a séance and there were people involved that were skeptics. They were supposed to have been screened. Unnoticed, they were planted there to debunk the demonstration. In the middle of the séance, one of the plants pulled out a flashlight and directed it towards the front of the cabinet thinking it was fake. The people fled away in a car that was waiting outside. Rev. Roy went into a state of shock. The ectoplasm snapped suddenly back into the solar plexus with great force. It was difficult trying to bring him to consciousness. He suffered for quite some time from this discourse and never did give another demonstration.

Apport Séance

Reverend Roy did do an apport séance at our center in Fort Lauderdale, Florida. That was an experience! We had a group of people sitting in a circle. The more people, about fifteen, gives the room more energy. The spirit chemist draws the energy from the sitters, it helps to produce this type of phenomenon. An apport is a semi precious stone.

A prayer was given before the actual demonstration. Reverend Roy went into a deep trance. We had a lovely meditation communication with our loved ones, spirit doctors and masters. We were very fortunate to have a Universal Master Teacher come through to give us words of wisdom. As I mentioned before, Rev. Roy was a direct voice medium also. The spirits of loved ones and teachers were able to utilize the molecular structure of the mediums body and vocal cords to produce phenomena. During the séance, one of Rev. Thomas Clarke could hear and see a crackling sound like lightning coming through the air and then it hit the floor. This special apport was given to one in the circle. Well, you say, how is this done? The spirit chemist can disintegrate the object, brings it through the atmosphere and it again becomes solid. It is extremely hot to the touch and you need to be careful how you handle it, because you could damage it.

Many people probably have witnessed an object that has materialized to them and wonder where it came from. I know my girlfriend Susan has had this experience many times.

Experience Five

Spirit Photography

One of the evidential phenomena was called Spirit Photography. It takes a lot of time and energy to develop this phase. At one of the Spiritualist camps there was a medium named Reverend Robert Chaney who had the gift. Mom made an appointment to have a spirit photograph done and I went with her. Rev. Chaney's room was set up as a dark room and had one of those old fashioned cameras that you see in an old western movie. There was a stool with a screen behind it. Mom sat on the stool and was asked to look straight ahead. Rev. Chaney's stool was set a few feet away from Mom. He put the camera plate into the camera, then covered his head with a black cloth and used a clicker at the end of a long string to snap the photo. Rev. Chaney was a clairvoyant medium and could see the ectoplasm being built up around Mom's head. He could see the spirits forming in and throughout the ectoplasm. When he felt he was ready, he snapped the picture. Like a photographer, he had to develop the plate. We were told to come back in one hour. There were spirits that had formed and Mom recognized one of them as her sister, Laura. Another spirit was thought to be my mom's teacher and one of them mine. None of the souls were living at the time of the photo, all were departed.

The actual photo may be seen on the cover of this book. This is the original photograph taken by Robert Chaney who was the co-founder of Astara.

Field Experience Six

Great Grandson of Geronimo

We were so fortunate to have had so many wonderful mediums to serve the church. I remember we had a guest who was the great grandson of Geronimo. Morgan was his first name (Morgan Eagle Bear). He was a clairvoyant and rather a large person. We had quite a large crowd, about one hundred fifty people, more than we were supposed to have. Naturally, it got very warm in the room. He turned to Rev. Thomas (my husband) and said "Can't you turn the air down?" We told him we had it as low as it would go. He then said "I'll fix this" and took out of his bag the most beautiful conch shell I have ever seen (it was from Australia). Morgan then took some sage from his bag, lit it and put it in the conch shell. After saying a few Native American chants, there were a few last minute people who came into the chapel and we were at standing room only. They approached Reverend Thomas and asked him if he would turn the air up, they were freezing.

The story he told us that evening was about a quest he was doing in his life (Native American terminology). He was training to become a chief and one of the quests he had to do involved hooking breast tips off of other Native tribes. They would hook each breast tip and tie a rope to it. He would pull until the tips were removed. Morgan had done three sessions of rituals and had three more to go. He told us the last one he did wouldn't work, so he brought two hefty tribe members and had them football tackle the person until the hooks came through. If you have ever seen a movie called "Hass" with Richard Harris, you would see a similar situation he had to go through. We did not keep in contact with Morgan and wondered if he ever became a chief.

Experience Seven

Can God Fill Teeth?

After we opened our center, Rev. Thomas, myself and a few others decided to go to a Spiritualist church. They were having a guest healer, who was quite well known. He has since passed on his name was Reverend Fuller. "Can God Fill Teeth?" was his heading. I thought it was interesting, I had to witness this. We arrived about the time they were going to start the healings. Of course a prayer was given per usual. The people were lined up on each side of the room.

Rev. Fuller would start at the front of the line and lay his hands on each sides of their face saying prayers as he went down. Bill, who was in our group, decided to get a healing. He said there was a strange feeling inside of his mouth that he couldn't explain. It had a metallic taste. He checked his teeth and found a fresh filling in which he had never had. A lady that was sitting in front of us let out a scream. She asked if anyone had a mirror so I handed her the one I had. "I have a new filling in my mouth!" she exclaimed. She had just been to a dentist and he told her she had quite a few fillings that needed attention. Long story short, she didn't have them done since she couldn't afford the price.

Following the healing from Rev. Fuller, she went back to the same dentist. He said, "Oh! You went to another dentist and had the work done? By the way - he did a good job on your fillings!" She told him she did not go to another dentist. She looked up at him and said "Do you believe that God fills teeth?"

There were quite a few people who had work done on their mouth quite successfully.

Experience Eight

Healings

In the healing gifts, there has been many healings preformed at our center. This was because we were primarily a healing center. There is one that I can remember quite clearly. This man used to come to the center twice a week to receive healings. We would have healings before our services on Sundays and Wednesdays. Sometimes he would fall asleep. I often wondered why he came to the center and I soon found out why! For quite some time he stopped coming to the center. Then all of a sudden he came back, had gained weight and looked very well. I asked him why we hadn't seen him at the center lately. He said he had gone back to the doctor to have his sugar tested and the doctor told him his diabetes was completely cured. He had had diabetes for over ten years. The doctor told him whatever he was doing to keep it up!

We had kept records on people restoring their eye sight, hearing, fixing back problems and so many more. Each healing has its own story. In healing there are spirit doctors that are assigned to us and work through us. They give us energy from the Universal Spirit to produce the healing that is needed. Each doctor has lived at one time now as well as in their past lives in their own medical profession. For instance, we have an orthopedic surgeon that we call Dr. C who is in the outer band with other specialist. Each is called in when they are needed. The earth healer are the instruments in which the spirit doctors are able to work to bring these souls through. They help direct the healing energy to the physical condition of the one being healed.

He or she is trained as a chemist to assist both the healer and mediums that have physical phenomena. There is much to learn about the gift of healing.

I was fortunate to teach the nurses at the University School of Nursing in Miami, Florida. The nurses had to have a credited course of therapeutic touch (laying on of hands) before they graduated. Finally, the hospitals and doctors were becoming aware of Spiritual Healing by touch. In London, England, the healers are brought in to the hospitals to help the doctors in treating patients as well as assisting in operating rooms.

Experience Nine

Soul Mates

People always asked, "How did you meet Rev. Thomas?" It started when I was told by someone they had heard of this medium that was supposed to be an excellent clairvoyant. I thought I would go to her and see what she had to say. I needed to go to someone who didn't know me. Our center was quite well known at the time. I made an appointment with her and she was a natural psychic.

We entered a small room in her house with a card table to which she sat on one side and me on the other. She had an old pair of regular cards, which she used to give readings. She only used them as a front. I could tell they were only needed as a point of concentration. She definitely was a clairvoyant medium. She began to tell me she saw I was in front of a lot of people. I didn't give her anything to feed on, I said nothing, no conversation. She told me I would meet someone across the pond that had two children. This person would help me in the work I do. I would be married by the end of the year, the beginning of next year. In my mind, I thought to myself, I don't think so! Or should I say I wasn't ready for marriage. She also explained what he would look like.

After the reading, as time went on our center moved into a larger facility. We worked day and night trying to get everything ready. Finally, I said we needed to take a break and get some balance in our lives. A girlfriend of mine was also helping us with the center, so we decided to go to a club. They had a wonderful singer and also had dancing. She had to work that night and would meet me afterwards. I got us a table and waited until she came. After she finally arrived we were only there together a short time when a gentleman came up to me and asked me to dance. I accepted.

I noticed he had an accent, he told me his name was Thomas and he was from Wales in the U.K. We had quite a conversation and decided to meet the next morning for breakfast. I showed him around Ft. Lauderdale and he was interested in the Indian (Native American) culture. We even went to a Cherokee Reservation. I saw him a lot until he had to go back to Wales. He was on vacation at the time. We corresponded for about six months. My mother and father were collaborating their fiftieth wedding anniversary which was the first of January. I asked Thomas if he would like to come over for Christmas and their anniversary. He wrote back and said he had some time off for the holidays and he would love to come. To make another long story short, we were married by the end of the year and yes he looked exactly like what the medium had told me he would look like. To this day, thirty six years later, we are both doing our spiritual work.

Before he married Rev. Thomas had a dream about what I would look like. This was before he had come over to the States for the first time. He said when he came into the club he almost fell off of his chair. I was exactly what he saw in his dream. He was impressed to bring his divorce papers over the second time. If he would of done that, we would have been married here in the U.S. We were married in the U.K. A lesson from this is to pay attention to your dreams and listen to your hunches.

Experience Ten

Trumpet Physical Phenomena

We finally had opened our new center and by this time I had already told Thomas I was a minister. His reaction was to ask me what kind of faith I was into. Naturally, I said I was a Spiritualist minister and professed to tell him what I believed in. He was quite impressed and interested. I asked him if he wanted to attend a séance we were having at the center and he was very much interested.

We had a large crowd that day about twenty five people. The new center was in a warehouse that had quite a high ceiling with metal rafters overhead. I spoke to a well-known medium who had the gift of trumpet mediumship and asked him if it were alright to bring Thomas into the circle. He had to sit at the back of the circle. We darkened the room and had a prayer before we started.

There were two trumpets, one on the medium's lap and one on my lap. We sat next to each other. I was sort of a battery for him to give energy and to be a door keeper. All of sudden there was a tremendous gush of wind that went across the room. The medium's Indian protectors name was North Wind. Soon the medium went into trance and his spirit doctor came through the trumpet (a funnel oblong type of aluminum that came in three sections and acts as a conductor of energy). One trumpet levitated across the room and landed right in front of Thomas. He said he didn't need any laxatives after that. Both trumpets went all the way up to the ceiling and you could hear them hitting the rafters above. The séance proceeded as different spirits came through. Truly a demonstration of physical phenomena.

Experience Eleven

My Aunt Mae's Experiences

My Aunt Mae was responsible for introducing my parents and myself to Spiritualism. She told us a few interesting stories about things that had happened to her while she was a practicing nurse taking care of an elderly man in his home. One day she was sitting by the kitchen table and happened to look out the window to see a woman in all black coming down the sidewalk. She went to the door to see who she was. As she opened the door there was no one there and the woman disappeared.

Another time the cups and saucers were floating and moving around in the cupboards. That night she was in her bed sleeping when she was suddenly awakened. There was a spirit woman yelling and screaming in another language at the man that she was caring for. The woman then came into my Aunt's room. Being a spiritualist, she knew how to handle the woman. Mae told her to get out of the house and quit bothering her. She was later told that there were a lot of negative things that had previously occurred in the house. Aunt Mae finally decided to leave that job.

Experience Twelve

Another Psychic Surgery

This story actually happened. Our personal doctor was quite impressed when he had heard what had transpired. One of board members Bill, had rheumatoid arthritis and was on cortisone. He developed ulcers and was treated by the same physician we used.

One night when he was in his bed sleeping, he was suddenly awakened to see spirit doctors surrounding his bed. A spirit advisor spoke to Bill explaining why they appeared to him. They were there to treat his ulcers and the other doctors were there to assist in an operation that they were going to perform. The spirit doctors put him into a relaxed state to raise the etheric body (I stated this in a similar procedure during one of my other experiences). They would have to heal the etheric body first, then in turn it heals the physical body. Bill said there was a master healer who instructed the spirit surgeons. The master healer told Bill to rest the next day and he was to drink nothing but broth. He felt so much better and had no pain.

Time moved on, but Bill was still having trouble with the cortisone. He took it upon himself to fast and stop taking it. It had an effect upon his body and he was admitted into the hospital. While in the hospital he had to have some x-rays taken. In the x-ray room, the technician asked Bill if he had just had any recent surgeries. Of course, Bill said no. The technician asked "Are you sure? Because I see there is a scar here like you just had had surgery?" Bill didn't tell him about the psychic surgery that the spirit doctors did. The technician looked really confused and decided not to take any more pictures.

Bill's physician had spoken to the tech and saw some of the x-rays that he had done. Bill was back up in his hospital bathroom shaving when his doctor burst into the room asking what had happened during his x-rays. Bill proceeded to tell his doctor about the psychic surgery.

The doctor became very excited, because he had recently been studying Edgar Cayce's manuals (Edgar Cayce was also known as "the father of holistic medicine"). He knew exactly what Bill had just experienced. He wanted Bill to put his story into the Enquirer, but Bill refused.

Experience Thirteen

Karma?

My mom had to go into a care facility, which was run by someone we knew, before she passed on into spirit. It was a private home and Mike who had taken care of her, had adored my mother and knew what our belief system was. He knew my mother was a very fine clairvoyant medium. So to keep her mind functioning and alert, Mike would have her give little readings to others.

One day a man who was one of the caretakers helpers came to get a reading from my mom. She looked at him and tears started streaming down her face. She refused to give him the reading. Meanwhile, the helper wanted to borrow Mike's car. He told him not to, because the insurance had ran out on the car. The man decided to take the car anyways. He drove the car down State Road Seven, lost control of the car, hit a guardrail and was killed instantly.

Sometimes we can sense that something bad is going to happen, but we can't put our finger on it. In a situation like this, was it his karma?

A Gift of Levitation

A dear friend named Vera, who mom and dad had befriended at the Spiritualist church in our hometown, had the gift of levitation. We had a group of about six people that would sit in our meditation circle. Vera was one of us that sat in the circle. We were trying to develop our clairvoyant abilities as well as the gift of trumpet. We did reach the point where the trumpet would start to roll around on the table, but only when Vera was there.

Her husband Patrick normally didn't attend the Spiritualist church with her. When Vera came home from church, he met her at the door quite perplexed. He told her as he sat in his favorite chair, one of the ash trays moved across the room in midair to another table. He knew Vera was interested in this belief system. That convinced him there must be something to levitation.

When she was in the kitchen one day, there were several demonstrations of levitation taking place. We took it for granted because we understood what was taking place. I have met a few people that have experienced objects moving around in their houses. It can be a loved one trying to make contact or even a negative nature in the house. You can deal with it if you know how to control the situation. You can learn how to do this.

I am a psychic artist of guides and teachers. I drew a picture (coming from my spirit artist) of my husband's guide White Rose. We put a picture on a stand and surrounding the stand with American Indian statues. One of the statues resembled Rev. Thomas' picture of White Rose. We set her close to the picture of White Rose, facing away from it. During the course of time, the statue turned around and was facing the picture.

White Rose

Experience Fifteen

The Music Box

We sometimes find people who are skeptics. We had a good friend of ours who was really doubting Thomas. He was called away, because his mother was dying. Our friend was at her bedside, when suddenly from the closet he heard a music box start to play. He asked his mother what it was, she told him it was a music box given to her by his father (who was deceased).

His mother passed away right after the incident of hearing the music box. After the funeral, Rev. Thomas' friend and his wife returned to his mother's house. His wife asked him where the music was coming from. He then told her about what happened right before his mother had passed away. He became a believer.

Experience Sixteen

Psychic Artist

On Saturday, February 20 2016, I was working as a psychic artist at a Psychic Fair. A lady came up to me to have a picture made. I told her I usually do drawings of guides and teachers. I asked for her first and last name on a piece of paper to set alongside my easel. When my artist takes over (the same as automatic writing) he knows what spirit is coming through. It takes me at least thirty minutes to do a pencil sketch. So I asked the lady to walk around to kill some time.

I have no idea who is coming through until it starts taking shape. I said my little prayer to ask my artist to take over. This time as the picture started to take shape, it took the appearance of a young man. (I dare not question my artist!) I just let him do his thing. I finished the picture and meditated on the picture. I felt the lady knew him.

When she came back I asked her if she knew who he was. I proceeded to give her a message that I was getting from my spirit guide. She said her daughter had lost a child at a very young age and still has not gotten over it. So the grandmother said that the picture that came through looks like her grandson (which would have been the young man's older brother). Even when people pass at a young age, they still grow in the spirit world. Usually they are by one of their family members, perhaps a great grandmother or whomever. I told her this child was a very high soul and was with his mother sending her love and light.

The lady left with her picture and showed it to her friend who was waiting for her. The grandmother asked if her friend recognized the picture. She said "Yes! It looks like a picture of your grandson who is still living!" She said her daughter would be so excited about the message I gave her to know her son is around her helping with the health problems she is having.

My Spirit Artist

Experience Seventeen

Dreams

Another time I did another drawing of a spirit from my artist for a man, doing the same procedure as I did for the grandmother. Not questioning my artist that works through me. I drew this very distinguished looking man with a beard and glasses. When the man came back, I also felt as though he knew him. When I handed him the picture, I thought he was going to have a heart attack! I was a little concerned and asked him if he was alright.

He replied, "Oh yes! I have to tell you this! Almost every night I would have this reoccurring dream having a conversation with a man who is scientifically educated and beyond the knowledge of scientists today." This man who was having the picture done, was from another country. The town in which he lived in was desperate for drinking water. In the next dream the scientist came forward and told him what to do to open the water supply.

He remembered what the scientist said and went back to his country to do exactly what the scientist told him to do. It worked and they had an abundance of water from then on.

Experience Eighteen

Spirit Guides Protection and Help

This was a situation of a person being protected by her Spirit Guide. My dear friend unfortunately was married to an abusive husband who had a problem with alcohol. In this state he became a different person. One day, she told me her and her husband were in the living room at their home. He was sitting on the couch when out of nowhere he darted towards her. She believed in Spirit Guides and called on them for help. All of a sudden there came this great force of energy between them. It totally picked him up and threw him across the room and onto the couch. He couldn't believe what just happened to him. After that he was a changed man and never touched her again.

Another incidence that occurred was with a young lady who lived in an apartment building. There was a man who was asking her out and continuously bothering her. She kept refusing him and had no desire to go out with him. One night she was asleep in her bedroom when this person broke into her room to make advances towards her. She too believed in Spirit Guide protection. Her Indian guide appeared behind her bed. The intruder was so flabbergasted and became distraught.

She called for help and when the police were sent. The intruder kept asking them if they could see this 'BIG Indian' that was standing behind the bed. "Can't you see that Indian!!" he yelled. He kept repeating it over and over again to himself as they took him off in handcuffs.

This last situation happened to a medium that I knew. He was going to a city to give a lecture and was unfamiliar with the area. He was staying at a location that was a distance from where he was lecturing at. He started to walk to his hotel and somehow he got lost. It was quite dark outside at this time. Everything is different at night. He didn't recognize any of the surroundings.

Out of the clear, there approached this man and he would tell that my friend was in trouble. My friend gave him the address of the hotel and the gentleman said yes he knew where it was that he had to go. He walked my friend to his location and as he started up the walkway to the hotel he turned to thank the gentleman for his help. The man was nowhere to be found. (Beware of Spirits un-a-ware).

Healing Testimonials

This experience happened at our center in Fort Lauderdale while were having our evening service. Reverend Thomas was giving the lecture when all of a sudden he stopped. His spirit teachers told him to go to the lady that was sitting in the front row. (We were basically a healing center and known for many cures.) Rev. Thomas got off the platform and went in from of the lady. He asked one of our members to stand behind her, said a prayer and placed his hand on her forehead. Suddenly, she fell backwards onto the floor and stayed there for a few minutes.

She came out of the trance and looked up at the wall. We had a plaque on the wall which had the number of the songs we were singing at the service. She looked up and could read all of the numbers. She was not able to read them before the healing. She was restored of her eye sight – Truly a blessing from the Universal Spirit.

Experience Twenty

Demonstration of Trance Protection of Your Guides

As I have mentioned, my mother was a trance medium. We were having a meditation circle at our place. We lived in a two story building at the time. My father had a grocery store and our living quarters were on the second floor. My mom, a friend, my Aunt and I were in the circle. Mom went into a trance state of course, our teachers came through and so on. All of a sudden my mother's Indian protector came through. He told me to go to landing where the steps lead to the down to where the outside entrance was. He told us that my father was about to come through the door. I could hear my father put the key into the door. Before he could turn the key, my mother's guide told me to tell him not to come in because mom was in a trance (my dad understood this).

They brought my mother out of trance and she asked what happened. She felt a shock go through her whole system. If it wasn't for her spirit Indian intervening, it could have been much worse. I always tell my students they should know who their guides are before they attempt any type of trance. They protect you from any lower entities to come in. This is very important in your development of mediumship.

Another time of the guides protection was when Rev. Thomas was having a meditation circle. Before the start of the circle they always said a prayer, call their guides and teachers to their places and calling in the outer band. There were students in the meditation for their development. After they had time to share what they received in their meditation. Rev. Thomas would go into what they call Cataleptic Trance (dead trance). His doctor teacher would come through, giving the students words of inspiration.

One night there was an undesirable entity trying to come through. Rev. Thomas' Indian guide was trying to protect him, when all of a sudden this Samurai warrior pushed through and stood between Thomas and the entity. The warrior raised his sword and told the entity to leave. It worked and showed Rev. Thomas was well protected.

Banding Together

Dear ones, as we gather our forces among men,
The time has come for use to take a stance.
We of the angel world must gather our
forces to help one another.
In their desperate need to overcome the dire
need for all to unite in the peaceful ways.
In their quest as a nation to succeed in the plight to conquer.
The destruction that man has brought upon himself.
Joys of gathering our thoughts together.
To become a nation of one spirit,
A nation to unite each other for peace and harmony.

Stop and Listen

We of little faith know no tomorrow.
We pray and yet we are not listening.
Our minds are so cluttered with our own thoughts.
We sometimes don't hear what is given to us.
Our Masters of Light so close and near, hear them we pray.
Trying to reach us to answer our prayer, but we don't hear.
Take the time to stop and listen.
The answers are there for us all to hear.
Just stop and listen, we are there to answer
your thoughts and prayers.

Come With Me

Go to sleep my beauty.
For the time has come for us to depart.
Come with me where trees are like colors of emeralds,
Flowers of color bloom everywhere and
wheat grows like spun gold.
Come with me and speak to the Angels of Light.
To learn and grow with wisdom from
those who have the Book of Life.
Come with me to share the glory of their gifts.
So that we may share it, for all the world to hear.
Oh, come with me!

Rise Above Mans Greed

The time has come for man to stop their greed.
For a power much stronger has come to be.
Giving the direction to overcome and crush the greed.
What gives us the right to destroy each other's spirit?
A power so strong we can no longer resist.
For the souls of man shall come to their knees,
Humbled to this power that is beyond our wants and needs.
A greater force that shall rise above the
greed, into a more spiritual need.
Love one another as the Book of Life is given in need.

Future of the Golden Light

End of the world, they say,
A beginning to the end.
Entering a new way of thinking.
Destroying the negative energies and vibrations of the old.
Taking on the spiritual thoughts of a higher consciousness.
Bringing forth of the ones who will teach us.
Not to destroy one another physically, mentally and spiritually.
Respect each brother for what he is,
regardless of race, color and creed.
In knowing we will become a believer of
a one spiritual, collected group.
Like a tree climbing, from branch to branch.
Cautious how we get to the top.
Careful of not slipping and falling when we get to the trop.
Eventually when we get over the top and beyond,
We are never asked if we are Catholic,
Protestant, Jew or more.

How Many Life Times?

Can this be a time of peace when we
can no longer have respect?
Who gives us the right to put a soul down?
Can we only realize we are responsible
for the deeds we preformed?
Knowing another lifetime to come.
We must face these souls again.
Making up the wrong we have done.
Over and over again, we come back until
we get it right with God and Man.
How many lifetimes will it take to have the patience,
love and harmony to bring us all together again?
How many lifetimes – how many lives?

Life's Experiences

Let it be known to all that hear.
No tears to be shed though out the years.
Our lives are planned to reach our goals.
Our lives to come will know our course by
being what we were led to learn the most.
Keep that thought and you will know.
That all life experiences has come to know.
Every deed is meant to be throughout eternity.

Clouds of Fear

Let thy light so shine into nature's growth.
The light that is ever reaching.
The clouds that hover above us at all times.
Is only our own misgivings of time.
Misgivings of nature's own meaningful depths.
Of Gods natural law sometimes not understood as yet.
We live and learn and grow with each step.
Rising above our own depths to conquer these clouds
of worry and fear.
They are only stepping stones to that
valley of inner peace from fear.
Most of all, to that Universal God's light.
Ever reaching, ever reaching, near.

Why Me God?

"Why me God?" have heard near and far.
From mouths of those who put to blame.
Not of themselves who choose to learn.
The blame to God! Who gives compassion and concern.
Can this be of Earth's souls who know no shame!
How sad we are to blame for our own mistaken identities.
Take recognition to your souls, which are to blame.
Seek the spirit within that,
Know the different of love not blame.

I Am Who I Am

My words are brought to light my soul.
For I am the seer of your faith and guiding light.
The guidance of your thought, may seem not understood.
To dismiss your life's work is not the
completeness of your destiny.
For I come to give you wisdom and
truth, for all the world to hear.
It is I who conquers.
Life's work in those I choose for all to hear.
Who Am I! That spills these pearls of wisdom.
I am the Spirit! That Universal Light within.

One Kindred Soul

The leaves turn green.
The flowers bloom in spring.

Where do we begin our lives, from there on in?
The rivers we have crossed.

The mountains we have climbed.
Oh soul our kinship becomes our destiny.

To fill our life's responsibility, from time gone by.
Our love has lasted through trial and error.

We still remain – one kindred sort – one kindred soul!

Eagles Fly

Soar above the Earth,
In flight to dwell into heaven's door.
Seeing nature's creatures that are no more.
Their souls still go beyond to their place of light.
Each in their own direction and goal of that light.
Reaching back to those they gave comfort to.
Still protecting and comforting with
unconditional love that still remains.
Like eagles in flight each come to know,
Freedom, to dwell in their way of life beyond the vail.

Who Am I?

In the upper chambers of,
In mediation I ponder.
Who am I when they say, you are of God likeness.
Likeness of a Universal Light that expresses only
Love, compassion and grace.
Not a wrathful God, or a jealous God,
That some men preach about.
Am I the true spirit that encompasses
what the true meaning of God is?
Am I capable of becoming that oneness of light?
Lifetime after lifetime I will one day become who I really am.
When the angel will say,
Yes, my child, you are a part of that Universal Light!

This Time Around

I choose you to be where I am today.
What is my purpose in the time today?
Is it karma whomever I am in contact with?
To work out trails of time gone by.
Perhaps to help a soul to overcome their trials today.
We choose the family to whom we unite, from times gone by.
No understanding until we finish this lifetime around.

Set Me Free

Set me free from the world of old.
Give me strength to carry on.
For my conscious mind has been at time a holding block of temptations.
Can I be strong enough to overcome the
negative ways to this world?
At times I feel the strength of those unseen forces close to me.
Guiding, protecting me in the direction I am to be.
Set me free to be what I need to be.
A soul of higher thoughts, forgiveness, love, compassion.
Just as the image of our God; was told us to be.

Rising Above Earthly Desires

The time has come for all to hear the words of what will be.
The world of peace, harmony and love.
The right to be free.
Can we of one spiritual energy, which we all emerged from,
Take control of our senses to realize each
of our responsibility to one another.
Can we respect each other as we would like to be?
Rising above the Earthly desires of power and claim.
To the harmony that we need within.
To recognize the Universal Spirit that dwells within.
Wake up world! The time has come for us to say,
What have I done to make this a better place to be?

Heavens Gates of Light

We speak of gates that open.
To heavens way of Light.
To worlds of existence that are beyond our normal sight.
We see that world by pleasure of delight.
Colors glorious that beam beyond the brightness,
Of the shimmering stars at night.
Valleys of green shown through prisms of glass.
Each cascading the colors of the sphere.
I, my soul, knows that place.
Can I work to reach that one glorious light of space?
Search inside and ask yourself.
Dear Soul, do I deserve that fate in my life,
When I reach beyond that light?

Going to the Light

Go to the light my soul, to seek.
For I know not what is beyond that vail.
Is it paths to go where ever I have chosen to be?
Is it a grandeur, bless and peace I seek?
Is it friends and family that we meet?
Depending on how we choose to be.
Our conscious mind we sometimes cannot control.
For what we choose a direction that is not a goal.
To places and stages of gray not to dwell.
Our spirit cries out for a higher goal.
We must take control knowing this is
what we are reaching for.
While here on earth we try to learn, expecting our challenges.
Teaching others through song and tales.
After all is accomplished thru trial and error.
When earth days come to an end.
Our souls are called beyond.
To a place where we have developed in the now end.
Will we have earned that place of grandeur,
bless and peace beyond that vail?

Angels in Our Path

Each corner of the world, we sit in different places.
Each one of their own experiences
and thoughts in their places.
We who dwell in the higher places seek
forth your thoughts and embraces.
Those that reach to Gods plan of life, know
no path of world's devastation.
They are the light and way for all souls misfortunate.
Compassion and love will guide in the faith
for those of little understanding.
Oh, Children of Earth we cry out in truth.
Expression of love to feel each being.
Your needs we hold in our souls so near.
Guiding and lighting each step of the way.
Come forth my children, for we shall help!
Make your path a ray of light.

Death Is Not an End

Death is not an end.
Only the beginning to an end.
Grief not for my soul.
Who waits on the journey's end?
Another dimension I have taken.
Going forth to greater lessons.
Picking up where I left off.
One to fulfill my life's intention.

One Stepping Stone

In life's road, passes many trials.
Some that are brought our way.
We sometimes don't attune to this growth,
In our pattern of life.
Journeys we endure with love, in this forwardness
Of our progression of life.
Those that have profited in caring of loved ones.
Have fulfilled and passed beyond their duties performed.
One stepping stone we have overcome
knowing a job well done.
Not looking to that past of loneliness and neglect.
Seeing a reflection of our image that we succeeded,
With God's light in this completeness of that one
Stepping stone of life.

Big 4-0

When we reach 4-0, life begins "they say",
We grow in wisdoms on our path of life, tis true.
Most of us who have reached that time, can only say.
Ye! Gads! Look at the gray hairs coming through.
Our weight drops here and there, mostly there. Oh! My!
We look back on days of old, when life we had, no care.
Times have come and gone when we reach that big FOUR-O.
Life becomes better I think! In 40 years we choose to go.
Good times, bad times, it's not so bad when we think of
Reaching the big FOUR-O.

Reach Out

Reach out to those that comfort you,
In ways of our minds we turn to.
The unseen forces that know your every move.
It is Universals way for you to seek,
The hopes and dreams in your life's stay.
We need to focus on those dreams,
Beyond our conscious mind.
Through meditation and prayer each day.
We can reach to seek our destiny in every way.

Final Words from the Author

I hope in some way you have had an eye opener while reading all of these experiences that I have shared with you. To learn over and beyond the old traditional ways you may have been taught. There is so much to learn in your lifetime. You can also develop these abilities in a spiritual way. Learning and using the gifts you were born with that possibly have been laying dormant. Your soul knows your utmost feelings. It is up to you to follow your inspirations, your hunches and your old gut feelings.

Not to ignore what your feelings are and not being afraid to experience what you truly believe inside. Something beyond what you were taught. I knew it at a very young age and thank God I had parents who understood as well. Be your own spirit, don't try to have people tell you any different. You are your own judge. The old saying is "judge ye not, lest ye be judged".

If there are stories in this book that may trigger your psychic remembrance in some sort, don't suppress it. Study it and reach out for the answers that haunt you. Search for a teacher of Metaphysics who will teach you in the correct way. Directing you in the path which is suited for *you* (like attracts like).

Knock! And the door shall open unto you. Ask! And you will receive. My greatest saying is when the student is ready, the master will come. Keep searching until you find the right teacher.

I leave you with these thoughts. It has been my pleasure to share these experiences with you. "Bless" you in your adventure to open up your inner feelings and beliefs.

In Light and Love,

Rev. Mary Linn Clarke

Printed in the United States
By Bookmasters